MW00390551

This Notebook Belongs To

____

Made in United States
Orlando, FL
11 December 2023

40599951R00068